"*Paper Hearts* is such a hopeful and heartbreaking book, with wonderful insight into the heavy truth of love. Lauren Jarvis-Gibson captures the experience of the falling and rising from the wreckage enthrallingly in this lovely anthology of poetry."

—Nikita Gill, author of *Your Soul is a River*

"*Paper Hearts* is an honest collection of poetry by someone who has dedicated themselves to living their life through their heart. Lauren is the kind of person who opens her soul to the world, and you can see that on every page of her book. This book is a testament to all the people in the world who have been hurt, but who still choose to love, and love deeply. *Paper Hearts* is honest, just as much as it is real. It is relatable, and it is filled with lessons any healing human being will find soothing, and encouraging. This collection of poetry will inspire your soul while healing it at the same time."

—Bianca Sparacino, author of *Seeds Planted in Concrete*

Paper Hearts

Paper Hearts

LAUREN JARVIS-GIBSON

THOUGHT
CATALOG
Books

BROOKLYN, NY

Published by Thought Catalog Books, a publishing house owned by The Thought & Expression Co., Williamsburg, Brooklyn.

First edition, 2017

ISBN: 978-1945796654

Printed and bound in the United States.

10 9 8 7 6 5 4 3 2 1

To the ones I have loved—

Thank you for giving me pieces of your hearts that I will hold so dearly in my own.

Thank you for giving me a story to tell.

This collection of words,
of tangled letters
and napkin scribbles
started out
dedicated to you.

And you're right that
I loved you
and perhaps those other guys too,
but this isn't about that anymore.
This isn't about you.

These words are my diary
my red heart screaming
and buzzing out loud.

These words are my soul.
My soul that has been broken
but is still somehow beaming
and blooming all the same.

These words
are me at 17 and 24
in the middle of falling in love
with a boy who left
and at the start of falling in love
with myself.

So you see,
this book isn't about loss at all—
this is about the start
of finding one's own self.

This is about the start of me.

And now, dear reader, it's about the start of you, too.

Before you fall in love

Before you fall in love
make sure to tie a ribbon
around your heart

just in case you unravel at his smile.

Before you fall in love
make sure to strap on your bulletproof vest
and bubble wrap your chest

just in case you hit the concrete.

And before you fall in love
make sure to brace for impact

just in case you lose your mind.

When a heart becomes a home

You were floorboards
always catching me when I stumbled over past mistakes.

You were the shutters on my roof
shielding me from the worst parts of myself.

You were my stained-glassed window
closing the blinds on demons I liked to make up in my mind.

You were my cabin
in the woods.

My house
away from chamomile tea and my mom's warm hugs.

Tell me
how I could ever forget
a boy like you.

Tell me how.

First love

I never knew my heart could hold so much.
That my heart could hold a fistful of fireworks in its cage
and a thousand stars glowing through every bleeding vein.

You changed everything I knew about myself.
You changed everything I knew about my heart.

It was you.
You changed everything I knew
about love.

You changed everything I knew
about me.

When I said "I love you"

I remember holding my breath
cradling the phone in my left hand
letting my tears fall through the speakers.

I remember not knowing how to say it.
Not knowing how to phrase it
dizzy on seventeen and broken rules.

I remember not feeling afraid anymore
when you whispered my name
and breathed in all of my hesitation.

All I know is
"I love you."
All I know is
"I love you more."

Baby, you were always meant
to have a permanent place
inked on my every bone.
You were always meant to take up space.

Midnight dreams

I stay up late.
Your name
like dried glue on my lips.

I'm scared to sleep.
Petrified your face will
leave my sight.

They say heroin
is the hardest thing
to quit.

But my love
you're the hardest drug
I'll ever have the privilege
to kiss.

Seahorses

August 12

Ruffled sheets.
I can hear the gentle exhales of your
breath as you sleep.
My eyelids droop
because I know tomorrow you'll leave
to go to a place
that isn't my bed.
That isn't your home.

August 13

I cried the sea for you.
Everyone shoves words in my mouth
but all I hear is your voice saying goodbye.
People tell me not to worry,
that there's more fish for me to catch
but we are seahorses, you and I.

And I don't know how to dance with anyone else.

We live on

Love will always have an afterlife.
It will always gleam in the clouded sunlight
despite the rain that tries to rust it.

Love will always live on.
It will always be stamped onto our beating hearts
making sure you feel his love
long after he walks away.

Love will always remain.
It will refuse to settle in the corners of your room
glowing proudly in the tiny crevasses of your soul
breathing long after your lungs give out.

Our love

Our love was always burning.
A perpetual forest fire
in a world where Christmas never ended
and you never stopped holding my hand.

Our love was always burning.

But we burned too brightly.
and nothing that bright
and nothing that mad
could ever last forever.

Love Story

A good love story doesn't have to end in happily ever after.
It's allowed to break and bend and burn.

Because what really matters
is the love that you found.

The love that you nourished.
And the love that you felt.

Not the love that you destroyed.
Not the love that left.

You are my perfection

What a simple realization it is
to know that while you may
never be the perfect human being
that you desire to see in the mirror,
you are the definition of
perfection
in someone else's eyes.

We aren't dead

Our love will always hang onto
the fragments I write at 2 a.m.

Baby, don't you see?

Our love still breathes
with every word that I exhale out of me.

17

I was just a girl.
But then you came along
and showed me that I wasn't ordinary.

I was just a girl with a
love affair with a minor chord
but you turned my soul into a work of art.

I was just a girl
until I met you.
I was just a girl
until you showed me that I was magic.

Wonder

How beautiful you are
to love someone like me
who finds devils in the sunshine
and angels in the rain.

My eyes

If you could look at yourself
through my eyes

if you could hear yourself
through my ears

if you could see yourself
through my rearview mirror

you'd know what love was.

Yours

I was never the image of
perfection

never the girl with the glossy
windswept hair.

But, my God,
when you looked at me

when you looked at me
with those ocean sea salt eyes

I swear I was yours
infinitely.

Soft hearts

Sometimes I worry
I'm too soft for this world

that maybe one day
I might explode from feeling
too much.

Always feeling too much.

I have to remind myself
that this world is full of
gray and glassy people.

I have to remind myself
that this world is full
of tin mans.

It needs more hearts
like mine.
It needs more hearts
like yours.

Held

You held my soul
inside your callused
hands

never questioning
the drums that hid beneath
my chest.

You said I was your moon
and you were my
Jupiter.

Can you see us dancing
in the sky
on Sundays at midnight?

I think back
to when you told me
that you would
never go

yet all I see now
is the sun
dropping beneath
the backyard trees
already on the run.

Already gone.

Lifeline

You were my heart.
Not just a piece
or a part

you were the whole
red, beating symphony.

my whole damn
lifeline.

Death seems so much
closer to me now.

You weren't supposed

to be the one to leave me with a bleeding heart
that only wanted a tiny taste of yours.
To be the one to crush me with just a word,
with just the whisper of a "sorry."
To be the one to rain down on me
when all I ever wanted was your shelter.
To be the one to run away from all that we had
when I was so tragically blinded by your smile.
To be the one I called my own
when you already knew I wasn't your destination.

And you weren't supposed
to be the one I called my home
when I was only a vacation.

I wish I could be more like them

I wish I could be more like them.
Like the ones from middle school
who never really had to try.

Or like the ones
who wear sunglasses indoors
and never apologize for it.

I wish I could be
the kind of girl that doesn't trip
over her own two feet.

Or like the ones
who take leaps
just to feel alive.

I wish I could be more like
the people who kiss other
lips without hesitation.

Or like the ones
that
love without thought.

I wish I could be
more glossy
more shiny
more cookie cutter.

More like someone
who doesn't feel the need
to care so much.

More like someone
who doesn't feel the need
to think so much.

I wish I could be
the kind of girl
that screams cool.

The kind of girl
that eyes swim to
when she enters a room.

I wish I could be just like them.
Caring less.
And feeling more.

Thunderstorms

You filled me up with raindrops.
that pounded on the window
watching us dance between white sheets.

Now you just fill me up
with my own damn poetry
forever drenched in your ghost.

First times

I was 15 and I said yes when a boy with green eyes
asked to kiss me on the escalator.
I was 17 and I said yes when the boy I liked
asked to kiss me after my show.
I was 17 and I said yes on the bed
when I thought he was forever.

I was 18 and I said yes when they asked me
if I wanted a second shot of something pink.
I was 19 and I said yes when they asked me
if I was lonely without him.
I was 20 and I said yes when they asked me
if I missed him desperately.

I was 20 and I said yes when they offered me free liquor.
I was 20 and I said yes to go to a surprise party in a tight silver skirt.
I was 20 and I said yes when the RA asked to call the police.
I was 20 and I said yes when they asked me if I said no.

You let our love drown

You were my sea
so I named you
captain of my ship.

You were my sun
so I let you have your way with me
and watch me tip and tumble
on the warm earth you handed me.

I always knew
you'd never sway me
in the wrong direction
that you'd never
steer me off course.

But then the waves turned their back on me
and the current pushed me aside.

I cried out your name
but was only met with silence.
I had no choice but to breathe in
your salty clenched fists.

You watched me
drown in the only place
I called home.

You watched my
love for you die
with the rest of my bones.

Drunk on the past

It's 10:36.
My sister moves out in a week.
My friends are getting rings on their fingers
and promotions and pretty little passport stamps.

I'm still here.

It's 10:36.
I'm stuck in the same routine
in the same state of mind and place
anxiously fluttering my fragile broken wings.

It's 10:36
and here I am again
wishing you were next to me
making it all better.

Making me all better.

Remnants of you

Seventeen.
My lungs are full of fresh air.
You helped grow them, you know.
I think you helped every organ
in my body sprout.
Maybe your smile was the
thing that planted my seed.

Twenty.
My lungs are full of sand.
It would seem as though they want to
die, just like my heart.
I don't think my body was ready
for the loss of you.
None of it was.

Twenty-three.
My lungs are clearer now.
I cough sometimes
still.
I think bits and pieces of
sand stayed in there.
Just as a reminder
you're still gone.

The day you left

The doctor says it's asthma.
The psychiatrist says it's anxiety.
My mother says it's the fumes.
'It's just the city smoke', she replies.
But deep down inside I know
that the day you walked out,
the day you told me to go
was the day I stopped knowing
how to breathe.

If you were here today

If you were here today
I'd soak you up like you were the sun
and I had a vitamin D deficiency.

If you were here today
I'd grab hold of your hand as quickly as I could
because years without the warmth of your veins
had me bleeding dry.

If you were here today
I'd give you every damn reason
just to stay.

Power outage

It's still light out
but all I see is
darkness.

It's still light out
but I can't seem to
find myself.

I try to turn your flashlight on
but the batteries died out
years ago.

I still bite my nails

Do you still carry my
messy scribbles on your heart?
I carry your fingerprint smudges
that like to drag my chest down.

Time moves fast
so why can't I rip you off of me
fast
like how you erased me?

Your fingerprints keep dirtying me
and caressing me with false light.
I try to wash you out of me
but scrubbing only makes me bleed.

What did I do to deserve your marks
on me that turn to rust
as my tears make their way
to you?

What did I do to deserve your
everlasting touch
that makes me itch and scratch at
the scab you formed?

You always told me to stop biting my nails
and to stop picking at dead skin cells.
I guess you knew I was never going
to break that habit.

I try to rinse you out with soap and water.
I dose my heart in bleach.
And even though it always stings
I like that you're still here.
I like that you're still something I can
constantly pick at.

Winter

Hearing your whispers in the wind
I cover my ears
and tell you it's only the cold
that makes me feel this way.

You know me better than most
and you tease and taunt me
making me wish for snow
to permanently freeze you out.

I think back to earlier Decembers
when all I needed was
you as my fireplace
to warm up my bones.

I think back to earlier Decembers
when all I needed was
you as my sweater
to cover all my ugly bits and pieces.

Isn't it funny how
seasons progress and
flowers bloom
but we are all still permanently
stuck at seventeen.

Isn't it a tragedy
to think that after all this time
I still long for the warmth
of your hand wrapped in mine.

When it rains in July

I used to plant gardens
on our grave
and water it with my faucet of tears.

By August
they shriveled into dust and
dried out promises.

Just like us.

Undress me

Baby
I need you to see my heart
and still call me beautiful.

I need you to see my soul
and still see pretty.

I need you to undress my chest
to see me naked in the daylight
and still see
love.

Friday nights

I fill up my lonely
with a bottle of $6 wine
hoping
that one day
it'll feel like your lips
on mine.

When you can't fix your own heart

You used to be the one
to stop these thoughts
that pop and hiss at me in the dark.

And now?
I have an orange tube filled to the brim.
And now?
I have too much red and too much rosé.

And still
I feel like I will lose my mind
without you here
without your hands
wrapping around my sorrow.

I asked my doctor what to do
but
there's no such thing as a pill
for heartbreak.

Blue

You once asked me why I only
liked sad music
and why I only wrote sad things.
You laughed at the thought of it
saying I was the only one in the world
with a love for blue.

Funny thing is
all I write about is you
and it's always navy blue and fogged up.
Your laughter still hums to me in the
background as I type in silence.

I can't write about you in watercolors now.
I can't pretend we are something that we will never be.
Still.
You are always glowing in the back of my mind.
You are always so goddamn blinding.

So for now, you are just a wash of primary.
You're a distant haze. A blur.
My fogged-up rearview mirror.
My wine stained journal.

Too bad I could never forget a blue like you.

Why did you leave?

When they ask you why you left her
tilt your head down and concentrate
on the soil beneath your boots.

When they ask you why you left her
bite your already short nails and try
to come up with a good enough answer.

When they ask you why you left her
listen to them call you a coward
and nod your head in agreement.

When they ask you why you left her
remember her crying as you shut the door
saying "goodbye."

When they ask you why you left her
feel a lump in your throat grow
and wish she were there to wipe your tears away.

When they ask you why you left her
think of her laugh and how she smiled at you
and forget the reasons why you ended it.

When they ask you why you left her
say the one thing that you've never said aloud
and tell them, "I don't know."

When they ask you why you left her
try with all your might to convince yourself
that she wasn't right for you.

And when they ask you why you left her
start from the beginning
and end with your biggest regret.

Second love

I wonder if she knows that
you told me once you would never love
anyone like you loved me.

I hope she never finds out.

Barefoot nights

My eyes grow misty
When I think about psychology class
and
JG-sized wine glasses.

I see you and me
and our midnight daydreams.
I see you and me
and our barefoot dancing.

I think about him and
my taped-up heart and all of the patches
that haven't healed yet.

And then I think
how lucky am I
to call you friend.
And to call that
love.

How lucky am I
to not need him
on the nights that I'm
with you.

I am a fool

I am a fool for you.
I try to color in the lines
and spray paint washes of you on my heart
but you always reply with
muted gray and off white letters.

I am a fool for you.
After all this time. Still.

My keyboard types away
Iloveyou over and over again
until my pointer finger grows numb
and I'm covered in your favorite shade of red.

I don't know why
my wilting garden mind
keeps replanting weeds
that you already clipped off of me.

I don't know why
after all of this time.
I don't know why.

On fire

My lungs are on fire
without you here.

I try to cry you out of me
anything to soothe the
scalding of my heart.

My tears are too hot
for my own good

and I am drowning
tumbling inside this drought.

I would do anything
to have you rain down on me.

Anything to stop this burning.

His hands

on the back of my neck
running an index finger
on every blue little vein.

His hands
clearing away
the rush hour traffic
in the highway of my mind.

His hands
already memorizing
the curves and the lines
he says he needs to taste.

His hands
on me
the closest
I have ever gotten
to believing in a higher power.

His hands
always hungry
frantic
unbuttoning
undoing.

His hands
fire and ice
striking his matches
our lips
heavy with sunset smoke.

His hands
always
burning me up
always
fucking me up.

Always making me
remember
that his hands
and his lips
don't exist anymore.

Always making me
remember
that his hands
are no longer
mine to love.
Not anymore.

It's weird because I'm happy

It's weird because I'm happy
But when I sit down to write,
the paper is sodden with blood
and the dust of your lips
on mine.

Is this what you did to me?
My heart is beating red
but my ink is black
and it's splattered all over
my bedroom floor
staining.

Now I can't even reach
out to anything
except for the words
you said
in regards to
"forever."

It's weird because I'm happy.
but when I sit down to write,
I only see your shadow
and the dried up prom corsage
you so carefully
collected.

My mind is a hollow tunnel.
I think you left me possessed
covered in your sweet stench.

Because what's left of you
is only the mess of me.
And what's left of me
is only the loss of you.

How does a heart forget?

I spoke to a friend yesterday.
She asked me almost innocently
how long it took for me to get over you.

I paused, with a shy smile playing across my cheeks
saying nothing and everything all at once,
wanting you and not wanting you all at once.

I say, "I never did."

Because don't you see?
You are the only thing I ever knew.
You are the only thing that I ever got to have.

You were not just a smudge
or a small ink splatter
running across my blood cells.

You were my whole immune system.
My sick days and my healthy days
My yellow days and all of the grays.

So when my friends ask me
for advice and for an expert opinion
on being whole on my own

how do I tell them that after all these years
you're still the only thing I could ever love
more than myself.

It's still winter here

The fireplace radiates warmth
from the top of my fingertips
to my tiny toes
yet
my heart feels chilly without you near.

Like it's lost its ability
to feel anything
but frostbite and
loss of circulation.

Like it's lost its ability
to feel anything
at all.

Undercurrent

My mind is an
undercurrent.
A sea
of "what if?"s
A wash
of endless question marks.
Please, someone.
Show me how to get out of my own head.
Teach me how to breathe
when the rest of me is drowning.

Let love leave

We never stop to think. Think about the consequences of our actions. Think about the hearts that we break without remorse. We only think of ourselves. We only guard ourselves because we're so damn scared.

We keep ruining things before they even begin.

We don't know how to do it. How to say goodbye to someone who we tried to give our hearts to. We don't know how to let it go. How to let that love run free.

We don't know how to say goodbye to something that was so close to being permanent. How to let that feeling go. That feeling of almost finding 'the one.' That feeling of almost making it to the finish line. And we don't know how to turn away from someone who we used to look at as our home.

So instead of slamming the door in their faces, we watch it slowly close from the wind. Instead of pulling off the band-aid, we slowly let it get washed away. Instead of saying "goodbye" we let it unravel in slow motion. We let the feelings slowly fade.

We become invisible. We pull away. Right when it's getting good.

We are so scared of saying goodbye, that we pretend it isn't happening. We shut our eyes. We cover our ears and turn off the lights. We wait for fate to take its course instead of taking control.

We wait until there's nothing left of that love. We wait until those smiles rust away. We wait until the butterflies collapse. We wait until there's nothing left to do, but to go. We wait until there are no remains on our bedroom floor. We wait until the love disappears.

We don't know how to turn that love into memories. We just let it die.

Maybe we're too scared. Scared of falling so hard that we forget how to breathe. Scared of loving too hard. Of wanting too much. Maybe we are all cowards. Cowards who say they believe in love, but run the second it comes our way.

Maybe we are just too afraid. Too afraid of rejection. Too afraid of loving someone so much, that we don't remember how to live without them. We are so goddamn scared of finding the perfect person for us. Because what happens when it goes? What happens when they stop smiling at us like they used to in the beginning? What happens when they get to know the real us? The ugly bits and pieces of us.

What happens when they say goodbye after getting to know who we truly are?

So we say goodbye before it falls apart. We slowly let the flowers shrivel up before August comes. We let love leave, just in case our hearts can't take it when we fall. When we fall and can't get back up.

First kiss

The second I kissed you
was the second
I lost myself entirely
to you.

Little did I know
how long it would take for me
to find my way back
to myself
long after you left.

Little did I know
how long it would take for me
to see happy
without seeing you.

Vancouver, Canada

I left a piece of my heart in Vancouver
between the skyscrapers and icy ponds
between the fireplace at your parents' house
and those tangled dirty sheets.

I left a piece of my heart in Vancouver
between the better days in January
and brighter days of March
between your toothy smile
and my mitten-covered hands always wrapped in yours.

I left a piece of my heart in Vancouver
between the rainy Saturdays
and vanilla lattes warming up our tongues
between the hungry kisses
and the photographs of us at 19 and 21.

I left a piece of my heart in Vancouver
between the chorus of "I love you"s
and the shouts about forever
between the whispers of tomorrow
and fears for next September.

I left a piece of my heart in Vancouver.
I can't get it back now.
I'll never get it back.

All Too Well

I have a love affair with the sounds of
minor chords that fill me up
in a way that you never did.

Home was him

I told him I wanted an
irreplaceable home
planted firmly onto the earth so
I could always run back.

He left that summer.

I wonder if he knows
that by 'home'
I meant him.

growth

You are only human

When you are hurting, tell yourself this. That you are only human. You are not made up of metal that refuses to break. You are not made up of concrete that can withstand the strongest of storms. You are not made up of the harshest wind that can knock down even the strongest of foundations. You are allowed to take a break. You are allowed to *feel*.

And when you are feeling sick with heartache, tell yourself this. That you are only human. You have one brain, one heart, two hands, and ten fingers. You were made to produce salty tears when your heart feels too weak to keep on going. You are made to feel with every bone in your body. You are supposed to ache with loneliness. You are supposed to feel everything that is terrible and everything that is beautiful.

Because you are only human.

And when you feel like you can't go on any longer, when you feel like you can't live another day, please remember this. You are only human. You break, you bleed, you bend, and you crack open. And yes, you are not made up of bricks that refuse to fall even during the darkest of hurricanes.

But, please, know this. You are made up of water, of the sea, that can drown the most terrible of feelings. You are made up of currents that can cleanse your soul of your darkest thoughts.

We say we are only human, and that we are weak because we

are breakable. But my dear, we all break sometimes, but we always can find a way to be reborn.

You have lungs that work day in and day out to give you inhales and exhales that you don't even have to think about. You have bones that protect your every muscle, enclosing your body in a safe haven. You have one heart that pumps blood throughout your body, and you have your brain, that makes you *you*.

You are human. But you are so much more than that. Because you see, while your bones and heart can break, while your lungs can weaken and your muscles can grow weary of this life that you live, your heart still beats. Your cells will still be reborn. Your lungs will still move in and out, no matter how tired you have become. Your bones will heal on their own, slowly but surely. And your body will begin again.

So while you are just a human, you are stronger than any natural disaster, than any army of wolves, than any man made metal, and than any tornado. Your body will keep working, even when you don't want it to. Your body will keep you awake, even when you just want to sleep forever. And your body will keep cheering you on, even when your heart has dropped to the ground in despair.

So when you feel like you can't keep walking, when you feel like life isn't worth living, and when you think that you aren't worth another day on this earth, just remember that you are human. Remember that you are mighty. You are the vision of strength and endurance even when you feel like throwing in the towel. And remember that you are beautiful, you are beautiful with all of your flaws and insecurities, even if you can't see it now.

Sweet human, you are a masterpiece of cells and bones and heartbeats. You are nothing short of a miracle, because you are here, breathing in this air and this life. You are nothing short of perfection because you are your very own person.

You are stronger because you are human. You are stronger because you have strengths and weaknesses, and you have insecurities and marks etched into your skin. You are stronger because you can break, and still get up the next day. You are stronger because you can die, and be reborn again. And you are stronger because, after all of the time, you wake up each day and continue to climb this slippery slope that is your life. And you must know that you are worthy of waking up each day and breathing in this beautiful and crazy world.

So please, don't stop climbing. Don't stop breathing. Don't stop living. Keep on going. Keep on walking. Don't stop trying. Don't stop inhaling. You are worth today. You are worth tomorrow. You are worth, a beautiful, masterpiece of a life. And you are worth giving yourself a shot to do more, to be more, and live a better life.

Always remember

Remember who you were
before he turned
your love
into a thunderstorm.

Remember who you were
before he threw
your heart
into the Pacific.

And remember.
Always remember
that you were a someone
before he ever
walked into
your wildfire.

Some day

They tell me so casually
that I'll find 'the one' some day.

"It'll just take time.
It'll just take patience."

I don't have the heart to say
I found mine years ago
but he didn't have the strength to stay.

You're still here

You were country air and city lights.
You smelled of mountain tops
and morning dew
covered in coffee stained flannel.

You were sunsets and sunrises.
Always too quick to leave.
Always too eager to show up.
Still—I held on tightly with my bare, tired hands.

You were the earth and sky.
You smelled of space
and gravity
that always pulled me towards you.

Now as the wind picks up
and as yellow leaves fall
on my boots you used to love
I only see your shadow.

You used to linger on my bedroom walls but
I painted over your fingerprints with my words.
You lingered on my window pane too
but I turned the latch to keep the cold out.

I only see your footprints this year.
They are dusty and a little bruised
but I still see them like I have for the past three years.
I still see you after all this time.
You're still here.

7-Eleven

You want me
when I'm dripping in gold
when my mouth is
full of only your favorite sweets.

You want me
when it's midnight and I'm sleeping
when you're hollow
from the bottles you've been drinking.

You want me
only when it's convenient.
But you were never just
a convenience to me.

No, you were more than
just a one-stop shop
for me.

Hearts can't tell time

Isn't it funny how
time changes everything
except for our love affair
with the past?

What were you thinking?

I guess that explains everything.
You can write a melody for me.
But I will always write the universe for you.

This is how you will learn to unlove him

Cry. Turn your bedroom into a raging sea. Into a tsunami that never stops damaging you. Into a waterfall that never stops running. Into a storm that never fucking stops punching you over and over again. Cry until you think it's over. Until you think your tears have all been dried. And do it all over again.

Scream. Scream into your pillow. Scream into his silence. Scream into your phone. Scream into the sunshine and into the rain. Scream until your voice breaks. Until you have nothing left inside of you. Scream until you lose your voice to call him up and tell him to come back. Scream until your head becomes dizzy and white stars fill your focus for a while, instead of him.

Sleep. Sleep in your bed that makes you feel so numb. In your bed that is missing his arms. His face. His legs. His touch. Toss and turn. Sleep through your alarm clock. Sleep through your classes until your roommates beg you to go. Then sleepwalk. Sleepwalk in the world where he left you.

Taste. Taste the way your tears fall. Taste your unwashed hair. And your sheets that haven't been washed for months. Taste his mouth on yours while you dream and wake up hungry. Taste other lips in search of someone that tastes like him. Taste their touch and their skin and remember that it isn't his. Taste too many glasses of wine. And don't just sip. Gulp it. Gulp until you forget. Just for a little bit. If even for a second.

Shop. Shop for things that hold no meaning to you. Give yourself a makeover. Hope that maybe a haircut will fix your heart. Or that a new wardrobe will cleanse him from your skin cells. Shop for things that make you look so pretty. So fun. So not sad.

Still be sad.

Talk. Talk to your friends. Try to laugh when they say they never liked him anyway. Let them hug you until you feel tears behind your eyes once again. Let them dry your faucet and let them hold you close until you stop shaking. Listen to them tell you that you're special and beautiful and he's an idiot. Try to believe them.

Wake up alone. Dry your eyes. Find pleasure in your dreams. The dreams that he is in. Drink another glass. Scream another scream. Talk another hour about how you feel so empty. Wonder when it's going to go away. This big black hole that has turned into your life. Wonder how people survive this. Wonder if you will die of a broken heart. Think about how that might be easier than living.

Recycle the tears. Recycle the screams and the wine bottles. Play it over and over again in your mind. Let days pass. Let months pass. Wake up. Go to sleep. Wake up. Go to sleep. Wake up. Pause. Breathe.

Breathe until breathing without him doesn't feel like you're choking on your own hurt. Breathe until inhaling without him doesn't feel like a knife inside of your throat. Keep going. Keep going until you learn how to be a human without him beside you. Keep going until you remember how to truly live.

It's your loss

You missed out on
the masterpiece of you and me
when you said goodbye.

Ghosts

I love so hard
yet
all I get in return
are
questions marks

blank spaces

silence.

I hope I left you with

the aftertaste
of peppermint and vanilla
from my lips on your chest.

the aftertaste
of Dior Addict and green apples
from my winter coat you liked to cast onto the floor.

the aftertaste
of all the words I whispered to you
that tasted like a promise I could keep.

the aftertaste
of getting drunk on love
and my outstretched legs all over your bed sheets.

the aftertaste
of red sangria and of "I love you"s
that still echo in your empty bedroom.

the aftertaste
of my salty tears and broken mouth
when you told me I had to go.

I hope I left you with the aftertaste of whiskey
when you remember
what you don't have anymore.

On the days you miss him

On the days you miss him
feel the tears drain out of your eyes
and hope to God he comes back to you.

On the days you miss him
feel all of that pain seep into your cells
and cling onto the thought of a failed forever.

On the days you miss him
flip through all the memories of him
that have been permanently etched into your mind.

On the days you miss him
let yourself weep, let yourself fall
and then let it all go.

On the days you miss him
feel everything and nothing and find the
strength within you to let him leave your heart.

On the days you miss him
say goodbye to all that you have lost, but
don't forget to say hello to what you have.

The day you leave her

make sure not to leave anything behind
because she will search her whole home
for anything that screams out your name.

The day you leave her
give her your most beautiful kiss
so that she will have one last piece of you
painted on her lips for forever.

The day you leave her
don't look back in your rearview mirror
as you pull away.
She will be standing in her driveway
trying to hold her heart together.

The day you leave her
do not call her weeks later
telling her you miss her.
She won't be able to hold
that kind of pain in her hollow chest.

The day you leave her
don't you dare come back.
Because even though she will wish
with every cell in her heart for your touch,
she knows she's better off alone
than ever being with someone who had
the audacity to run in the first place.

This is how you let him go

Turn the volume up
blast the stereo
until your ears begin to hum.

Drive
without a map
without an app
to take you back.

Roll the windows down
and smile at the guy on the street
who doesn't know your name
who doesn't look like *him*.

Take a walk down the park
the park that smells like his shirts
and hold your breath
so you don't have to inhale his ghost.

Fill your glass up
with something bubbly
something happy
that takes away the empty.

Write until
your fingers bleed
until your fingers
beg to let them off the hook.

Drink until
you're seeing stars
and shining eyes
and spin until his
face isn't what you want to kiss.

Eat too many
chocolate bars
and Ben and Jerry's and
laugh about how predictable you are.
Laugh until your bedroom becomes a sea.

Wake up the next day.
Do it all over again
until it hurts a little less
stings a little less.

Wake up the next day
breathe in your pain
and the hurt
and the empty.

Wake up the next day
and breathe it in
until your lungs
grow accustomed
to the sting.

Until your lungs
grow
accustomed
to his ashes.

He's not God

He had a beautiful smile.
He spoke in poetry and prose
that would put Shakespeare to shame.

He had a soft heart
and a way he said my name
that sent goosebumps to my hungry chest.

I used to call him love.
I used to call him destiny.
I used to call him church.

But he is only a boy. Remember that.
Just a pretty face
with a habit of getting under your skin.

Just a boy.
Not God.

Made to grow

I was born with a paper heart.
I flutter when everything gets to be too much.
I crumble at devastation.

I don't know how to not
rip apart at the smallest of things.
I don't know how to stitch myself back up
to how I'm supposed to be.

I was made to run out of breath
and to cough on broken promises.
To easily drown in puddles
that only rain boots were invited to jump on.

But I was also made up of black and white photographs
that my mother kept on her nightstand.
I was made up of California suns
that my dad used to chase in the dark.

I was born with a paper heart.
Fragile and weak
but cradled by stronger hands
that gave me the ability to live.

I was born with a paper heart.
bound by roots and branches
that gave me oxygen when my lungs
had no strength left in them.

I was born with a paper heart.
But maybe after all of this time
I wasn't made to tear or to break.
Maybe I was made to grow.
And maybe, just maybe
I was made to bloom.

Finding happiness again

I know you feel like you won't ever be able to believe in true love again, and that you will never be able to dust yourself off from the smoke he left in your heart.

I know you feel like sorrow is piercing every bone in your body. You feel it so heavily. It feels like every inch of you is on fire, and you just want to wash yourself away with alcohol, with drugs, and with other bodies. Just to feel something other than pain. Just to feel something other than nothing.

But here's the truth about heartbreak. Losing yourself in a vice is only going to prolong the hurt. It is only going to numb you until it hits you all over again. That bottle of whiskey, that naked stranger in your room, and that drag of a cigarette is only going to stunt your growth. And it is only going to slow your healing time.

What you need to do is to feel.

To feel the ripping and tearing of your heartstrings. To feel the crashing and burning of your once-true love. To feel the repressed tsunami erupt from your eyes, without caring about the flood you will ultimately create.

You need to feel all the hurt and all the pain, in order to come back from the dark and to one day find the hope that you will gain from this heartbreak.

You just have to keep surviving and learn how to keep living with this hole in your heart.

And after you have grieved, after you have burned his things and cried your lungs out, only then will you start to heal. Only after the destruction, will you be able to start rebuilding your heart back up again.

It will happen when you least expect it. A smile. A flicker of hope. A tiny moment where you truly and honestly feel happy. And even if this happens for half of a second, that is still something. That is still a flame of light.

It won't happen quickly. And it won't be linear either. But one day, you'll feel a stirring in your heart. You'll feel lighter. And you will want to smile again. Not for him. Not for her. But for yourself.

rebirth

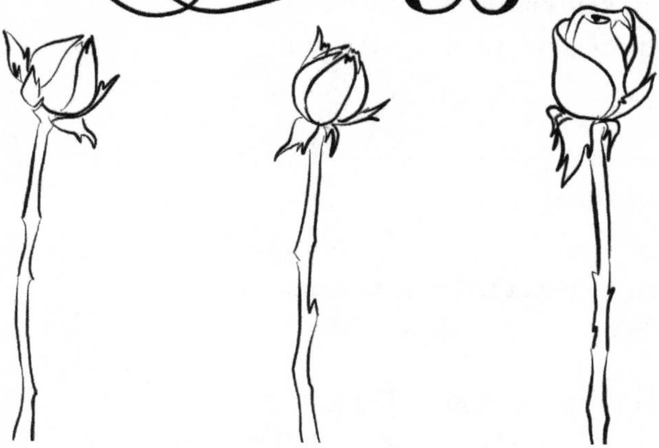

Spring's rebirth

Winter leaves dust on our shoulders
and goose bumps that last till March.
Ghosts from our past
show up in the snippets of sunlight
that our bodies can't reject.

But when the rain starts to fall
and handprints are washed away
from the pounding on our windows
we can't help but rise and recover
with the season that allows everything
to restart.

And when the grass starts to grow
and the bursts of Decembers past
gets knocked down from the sunlight of May
We can't help but wake up each morning
and smile up at the sunrise.

We can't help but smile at beginnings
and say good riddance to all that we have left.

Self-love

Love yourself
the same way stars
hug the lonely sky

Love yourself
the same way the ocean
kisses dusty sands.

Love yourself
the same way the sun
greets the dying dawn.

Amor

He calls me *amor*
and cups my face in his hands.

He sounds like my favorite song
I haven't discovered yet
and I can't stop hitting replay.

He tastes like fine aged wine
and cherry vodka
like something I never knew
I had to have.

He calls me *amor*
and for the first time
in a long time
it feels like home.

Evergreen

I tell them,
"It's ok."
I turned his love
into poetry.

I tell them,
"I'm fine."
I turned his leaving
into an evergreen.

Your shipwreck

I never thought I'd meet someone
who could make me forget
about his shipwreck.

That I'd meet someone
who could make me
remember that my heart is
still alive.

Who would help me remember
that he did not suck all
the honeysuckle from my
veins.

And that a boy
who doesn't resemble him at all
could make me taste
love
all over again.

Your pain

Your pain
isn't always
black and white.

It will live inside
your bones
and crack wide open without
ever asking for permission.

Your pain
will always stay.

Your pain
will always breathe.

And that's okay.

Maybe
that's the point of life.

To live
even when it hurts.

Keeping us alive

I've never been the best
at taking care of
me

but I've always been the best
at keeping
you alive.

I've always been the best
at making sure
our love
would never be forgotten.

Made to love

Do not be afraid.
For you were made to love
as your heart was made to beat.
As your lungs were made to breathe.
As your eyes were made to see.

Brooklyn

I took a trip to New York City
remembering how we used to
call it ours.

How silly we were to call it home
because a city of stars
were never meant for two.

I took the train to Brooklyn
and turned the nostalgia
into noise.

I turned your memory
into Manhattan
and poured your ghost
into my glass.

Red light

You whisper, "red light,"
and take your hand off the gear
placing it on my face instead.

Kiss me and call it love.
Just for tonight.

You whisper, "red light,"
a smile creeping up on your lips
while you watch my face burn too brightly.

Kiss me and pretend it's destiny.
Just for tonight.

Kiss me and call me yours.
Just for tonight.
Just at every red light.

My lonely

Loneliness seeps in
begging to be loved
begging to be touched.

I keep on kissing mouths
I should have never tasted
and never should have trusted.

But there it is again
that hollow beating in my chest
shouting at me to be held.

Always shouting at me to be let out.
To stop being so afraid to fall.
To stop being so afraid to love.

The eye of the storm

I was the hurricane
you never could outrun.
The wildfire
you never could put out.

I was the eye of the storm
you gladly jumped into.
The tornado
that rushed you away.

I was the thunder
and the lightning
you never could get enough of.

But all I did was rain on you.
All I did was watch you burn
All I ever did was watch you fall
and let you break.

I'm sorry.

Your current

I used to be so afraid of drowning.
So afraid of my lungs
getting soaked up in a wave.

So deathly afraid of my heart
becoming sand.
Of the ocean taking every
last exhale from me.

But baby
I'm not afraid anymore.
All I want to do is drown in you.
All I want to do is collapse
under your current.

Recycling bin

I am more woman
than you will ever be
man.

You shushed me
and complained that I
sucked the honey out of you.

All you ever did was whisper
with your cracking voice
barely bruising my beating chest.

So I left you
deaf and shaking
with my heart heavier
than the weights you lift.

So I left you
mute and confused
with your heart
balled up in my fist.

You were always
too easy
to crumple up and toss
away.

Go

Go until you forget who you used to be.
Until your past turns to patched up scars
and hazy midnight drives.

Go until you forget
what fear is supposed to feel like.
Go until you forget how to break
and remember how to heal.

Our ashes

I always thought that
you would turn me into ashes.
That your loss was too much
of a burden to bear.

But here I am still
beating breathing believing
in something greater than our love.

Here I am
still pounding on our grave
with a fist full of flowers instead of tears.

Here I am
so ready to bloom
in ways that would leave you blind.

Here I am
growing wildly
and all the same
still so hopelessly in love
with how you loved me.

24

I guess I thought
I would have it all figured by now

but
the boys who cried wolf and
the friends who turned to
ghosts
are still a mystery to me.

I guess I thought
I would have been more prepared at 24

but
here I am still aching for their love
still reaching for their hands
to hold

always, always wanting answers
always, always wanting more.

Drink up

I'd like to think that
the tears you wept
from the loss of me
overflowed the rivers
in your hometown.

That the tears
you shed for me
found its way back
to the water I drink
in May humidity.

It's nice to think that
your regret
could quench my thirst
and nourish my
every
single
cell.

I'm ready now

It's miraculous
that my bones still heal
and my wounds still scab.

It's extraordinary
that my blood still pours
and my voice still shouts.

After all this time
my body is
still capable
of holding so much hurt

and all the while
still so ready
to jump into
other hearts and bodies.

I'm still so eager
to feel every beating
and every blooming
the world has yet
to place in my hands.

Begin again

Never stop reminding yourself
that you are a human being.

That you are not steel
or armor
or man made weapons.

That you are allowed to
flood the oceans
and break the dams.

That you are allowed to
rust and shake and
bend some more.

Breaking is just
another way
to grow into someone new.

Breaking is just
another word
for beginning.

Empty ribcages

Your tears
are stronger than their
empty chests.

Your love
will never weaken
from their havoc.

Your worth
will never wilt
from their goodbye.

Do not let their mediocrity
win.

What you deserve

Never treat someone
with more love
with more dedication
and with more kindness
than you give
to yourself.

Growing roots

It's easy to believe
that you need someone else
to jumpstart your heart

that you need someone else's
mouth and eyes
to guide you while you climb.

It's easy to believe
that your body can't hold up
without the love that left you
flying.

But you cannot let their leaving
deplete your oxygen.
You cannot let their leaving
and their fear of love
clip your already growing roots.

Take it back

Turn their leaving
into your beginning
and take his love back
and feed it to yourself.

East Nashville

I'm in an olive green house
far away from home
but feeling more at home
than I have in a long time.

I'm 24 but I feel like I'm 16
Ari and I drink too much
Prosecco
and we laugh about boys
who we used to love.

My rib cage is full
and my heart isn't blue or cold
or empty anymore.
It's Tuesday and I am so alive.

I don't want to go home
or go back to him
Here my heart belongs to no one
and my god I feel so free.

I am so free.

The beginning

Your story
has only just begun.

And you—
your precious heart
has only just awakened.

So promise me
that you will live
Truly
Deeply
Freely
Live.

I'm alive and so are you

Breathe.
Know that right now
You are alive.

And even if you are hurting
know that this feeling
Is only a passing moment.

Please
never take
your inhales and exhales
for granted.

You are alive
and my God,
even in the dark
I can't help but shout out,
"This life is so beautiful!"

And so are you
And so am I.

The race to nowhere

We are told to run at full speed
to be the one to leap the highest
to be the one to go the furthest

but we are never taught to just be
we are never taught to just breathe.

And maybe after all of this time
instead of having to fight to survive
and instead of having to collapse
under our own weight

we should learn how to live.
And to just be.
Just be.

Butterflies

I haven't felt them in a while.
But then I saw you.
And I felt it.

The stirring in my stomach.
The waterfall of wings.

I saw you
and my tongue forgot
to remember how to speak.

I saw you
and my heart remembered
how to beat.

I just hope to God I haven't forgotten how to fly.

Without your soil

Years without your nourishment
I stand tall.
I don't droop anymore.
I don't wilt with you
on my back.

I stand straight.
My spine aligned and
all my petals intact.
I don't need your water
anymore.
I don't need your soil.
I grow on my own.

This is how I became happy without you

I kept on living.
I kept on breathing shallow breaths
until they weren't so forced anymore.
I kept on taking baby steps
until they weren't so small anymore.

I talked. I wrote. I walked. I ran. I grew.
I just lived until living without you
didn't seem so bad anymore.
I lived until I was content.
with just me.

Your worries

Do not let the skyscraper
of your worries
blur your vision with the dust
it rains on you.

Don't breathe in the noise
and the fumes that your mind
tries to suffocate you with.

Know that you can outrun your demons.
And know that you are stronger than
any darkness that tries to ruin you.

It's okay

I whisper to my heart,
it's okay love.
It's okay to hurt.
You're allowed to break.

Promise me
you won't stop fighting.
Promise me
you won't ever stop.

Your wounds

Time doesn't heal wounds
to make you forget.

It doesn't heal wounds to
erase the memories.

Time leaves you with a scar
to remind you of how you fought through it.

Time leaves you with a scar
to remind you of how you bled

and how you survived.

You survived.

Kindergartners

Maybe after all of this time
we are all just kindergartners

searching for a purpose and
for a safe place to rest our tired heads on
when the world grows too dark.

Maybe after all of this time
we don't want the success or the fame
or the lust.

We just want to be found.

We just want to run home.

Your heart

I hope you know your heart
is a sacred piece of art.
That it's covered in blooming gardens
and August sun rays
sprouting throughout your chest
to the inner depths of your mind.

I hope you never give up on its ability
to prosper
even in a drought.
I hope you never lose faith
in its ability to be reborn
even after its death.

Run free

You're allowed to set yourself free
from the life you have grown tired of.
You're allowed to wave goodbye to those people
who do nothing but pour salt on your open wounds.

You're allowed to do something for yourself.
To escape the life that has trapped you in its grasp.
You're allowed to leave the dust behind you
and to not look back, if you don't want to.

Your light

Don't ever let someone
shake away your light
just because they are full of shadows

and don't ever apologize
for burning their eyes
when they have never seen the sun.

Thank you

Thank you for your goodbye
for
in your leaving
I gained a deep love for myself
that I never had when I had you.

Thank you for your goodbye
for
in your leaving
I gained me.

The love you deserve

Your heart is too big to accept anything less
than whole hearted love.
And it is too full of stardust
and life
for you to ever waste it on the moon
when you are and always have been
the sun.

Seagulls

You were made to fly, not to fall.
You were made to bloom, not to wilt.
You were made to prosper, not to crumble.

You were born to shine, not to shrink.
And you were born to rise like seagulls in the sky
not to sink along with the worn-out tide.

Nostalgia

Right now, your life is coated
in memories of boys who
bit your bottom lip too hard.

Right now, your life is bathed
in regrets of throwing them away and
In goodbyes you wish you could take back.

Right now, your life
Is an overdose on salt water
and splotchy skin you don't know how to soothe.

Right now, your life
is a tsunami of disappointment.
A hurricane of fear.

But right now is only a second.
Right now is not
forever.

Healing doesn't mean forgetting

Healing doesn't mean
he never existed.

Healing doesn't mean
love was never there.

Healing doesn't mean
you never cared.

Healing is
nourishing your fragile bones.

Healing is
finding beauty in the endings and allowing
your heart to open up to new beginnings.

Healing is
learning to love yourself
so much more than
the past that has already slammed its door on you.

Your tired limbs

I know you're tired.
Tired of trying so hard.
Tired of losing every battle you're in.

I know you think it isn't worth it.
That this life is too much
and too harsh for your fragile heart to carry.

But the world needs people like you in it.
People like you who never give up
no matter how much weight is placed upon your shoulders.

I promise you, we need you.
We need soft hearts and broken wings.
We need battle scars and hopeful wounds.
We need that kind of beautiful to stick around.

Forgiveness

Forgive yourself for causing your own heart pain.
For ever telling yourself that you weren't worth it
and for ever causing your own heart to break.

Forgive yourself for treating your own soul
in a way that you would never treat anyone else's.
Forgive yourself for being human
and for being strong enough to feel.

Secret garden

Just wait until she becomes
a garden.

Just wait until she grows
into so much more
than just being yours.

Maybe time isn't supposed to heal everything

I used to believe that time was my best friend. That time had the ability to fully erase the past. That it had the power to make me forget all of the hurt and pain my heart had endured.

I thought that if enough time had passed, my heart would be able to erase it all. Erase all of the heartbreak and the scars that love had marked on me.

But I have come to find that time isn't so forgivable. Time can't make it go away. It won't heal the scars completely. And it won't make you ever forget.

I used to wish so desperately that time would be on my side. I did everything I could to make the ghosts go away. I threw out old letters. I blocked people on social media. I disciplined myself to not talk to people who I shouldn't.

I cleansed my closet of old shirts and memories. I crumpled up pictures and polaroids. I did everything I could, to throw the hurt away.

But no matter how hard I tried, I couldn't block away thoughts of him. I couldn't block out the tears I cried or the flashbacks of first kisses. No matter what I did, the broken love still followed me. He still followed me. And I found myself still being haunted.

But then one day, as I was filled with nostalgia yet again on a beautiful fall day, I decided to stop. To stop running away from the hurt. To stop running so far away from the pain and from the past. I decided to let time do its thing, instead of trying to force it to make me forget.

And I stopped trying so hard to forget.

And when I stopped trying so hard to erase the past, I started to feel better. Instead of trying to mask my hurt from the world, I decided to greet it. I stopped running. And I started actually feeling.

And as soon as that switch turned in my mind, I realized that time shouldn't be something to heal every wound. Time shouldn't be the thing that we rely on to make all of the pain disappear. Because truth be told, life doesn't work like that. And love doesn't work like that.

If the love that you had was real, you won't ever forget it. You won't forget the memories. You won't forget him or her. You won't forget how your heart felt. If the love you had was genuine and real, time won't erase that.

And maybe that's a good thing.

Don't try to fight your healing time. Don't try to have a tug of war with the test of time. And don't try to forget.

You're supposed to remember it. You're supposed to remember and smile at the memories. You're supposed to know that at one point in time, you were magically and wonderfully in love. And you're supposed to know that at one point in time, someone held a piece of your heart and vowed to never let it go.

So don't try to pack up the pain. Don't throw out the memories and the drops of tears that you hold in your chest. Just let yourself feel. Let yourself remember. And let yourself fall in love with the memories.

You're allowed to remember it all. Because a love like that was supposed to be honored and cherished. A love as powerful as that was meant to be remembered forever.

Let go

You can run from your sadness
and hide from your fears.
You can shield yourself from the hurt
and push aside your anxieties with a couple of white tiny pills.

But you are going to have to feel it one day.
To feel the pain that you have held onto for so long.
To feel all the hurt that you have turned your back on.

Darling, you have to let it go.
You have to empty it out
and purge yourself of all the toxins you have over fed.

Only then will you climb with no weight on your back.
Only then will you smile without tasting ghosts on your lips.
Only then will you dream without ocean tears
blinding your sight.

Your tears

Let your tears water the roots planted on your feet.
Let your tears water the seeds sprinkled on your mind.
Let your tears nourish the holes in your heart
and let your tears know that they are welcome.

Let your tears feed the void written on your chest.
Let your tears soothe the rash
he left on all of your fragile little limbs.
Let your tears quench and fill the thirst of loving him
and let your tears hold your heart,
enclosing you in all the love that you have left to give.

Again and again

Don't ever stop believing.
Believing that your heart will prosper.
Believing that your heart will heal.

Don't ever stop believing.
Believing that big love exists.
Believing that love is worth it
even after it has gone.

Don't ever stop believing.
Believing that your soul is still made up of magic.
Believing that you are irreplaceable.
Believing that you will love
again and again
and again.

He is blind

Do not ever be with someone
who does not make
your heart feel held
and do not ever
give all your wildfire to someone
who is blind to your light.

I won't forget

I still remember when you slid my hands
inside your pocket to keep my piano fingers warm.
and the time you brought me
three different types of tea
because you forgot my favorite kind was black.

I still remember how you spread yourself so thin
to cover every broken crevice on my body
and how you never meant to hurt me
even though you did.

I still remember the way you smiled at me
when you showed your mom
the Tiffany ring that you bought me.

I still remember it all.
Thank God time never let me forget.

The absence of you

The absence of love in my heart
used to feel like freshly sharpened knives.
It used to feel like gunshots that never healed
and broken limbs that never recovered.

The absence of love in my heart
used to feel like lies.
like a betrayal that never left
my dehydrated wine stained lips.

But eventually
the bullet holes faded.
The broken limbs didn't need surgery
like all the doctors thought.

And I finally realized that
you were never the one I needed.
I just needed me
to fix myself.

Before the fall

We will never be fully whole.
There will always be cracks.
There will always be holes.

And as much as we try to fill ourselves up
with merlot and naked limbs
we will always end up with our hollow hearts on display.

We will always have the frostbite of December in our souls
and the heat waves of August in our hearts

Maybe that's why God created Octobers.

Skeletons in your closet

I hope you learn to say goodbye to
ghosts from your past.
To stop holding onto people
who loved you years ago
and to stop loving people
who already have let you go.

You deserve a life that isn't full
of skeletons in your closet.
A life that isn't full of blank pages
and chances you never took.

You deserve to live a life without
the demons that haunt your heart.
You deserve to live a life without
the people who took your heart
and cackled at your ashes.

Never stop looking

She is strong
because even in the dark,

even when the world is gray
and quiet

she still has the ability to see the sun.

Breaking and not dying

Isn't it wonderful to think and to know
that your heart can break a hundred times
that your heart can rip at the seams
and flood your bedroom floor

Yet it still won't ever leave you.
It won't ever stop beating
even when he is gone.

Isn't it beautiful to know
that your heart still lives
even after the death of love.
Even after the decay of your bones.

Isn't it a miracle
that your hearts still here
beating breathing burning.
It's still here.

You're still here.

Holding your hurt

You hold your hurt
like an organ in your heart.
You hold your pain
like a piano in your palms.

You need to stop
letting background noises
and elevator music
take up so much space
inside your paper mâché body.

You need to turn your pain
into your symphony.
You need to turn your pain
into your battle cry.

I'm alive and so are you

Breathe.
Know that right now
you are alive.
And even if you are hurting
know that this feeling
is only a passing moment.

Please
never take
your inhales and exhales for granted.

You are alive
and my God,
even in the dark
I can't help but shout out,
"This life is so beautiful!"

And so are you
And so am I.

"But still, like dust, I'll rise."

—*Maya Angelou*

Acknowledgements

Thank you to Chris, Mélanie, Bianca, Rania, Ari, Lacey and the entire Thought Catalog team. You guys are my family and I am so grateful for all of you.

To H, M, LC, N, V, E, R, NW, who lift me up when I can't lift myself up.

To my mom for showering me with endless amounts of love and support.

To my dad who always manages to cheer me up with a bad joke and a good beer.

To Jeanne, the Mary-Kate to my Ashley.

To the boys who will always take up space inside my heart.

And to you—thank you for reading, for breaking, for growing, and for living right alongside me.

YOU MIGHT ALSO LIKE:

Your Soul is a River
by Nikita Gill

In Regards to Forever
by Lauren Jarvis-Gibson

Seeds Planted in Concrete
by Bianca Sparacino

THOUGHT
CATALOG
Books

9 781945 796654